WOMBERG'S FRIEND ADVENTURE!

BY MAXWELL MOULDER

About the Author

Maxwell Moulder is a Northern New Jersey native. Max was diagnosed with autism at the age of 3, initially classified with PDD-NOS (Pervasive Developmental Disorder Not Otherwise Specified), later changed to ASD (Autism Spectrum Disorder). He didn't begin speaking until the age of 5. Initially, his parents suspected he might be deaf, which would explain his inability to speak. However, they soon discovered his autism. Max started school at 3 and received 1-on-1 speech therapy for 2 hours daily, gradually developing his speech. Max has faced his share of trials and tribulations. In August 2018, Max began attending Heidt Center of Excellence in Cincinnati, Ohio, making tremendous progress within the program. He graduated in May of 2024 at the age of 22.

Max has always enjoyed drawing and possesses a remarkable ability to convey profound emotions through his art, often without the need for words. Given his challenges in showing emotion, it's truly remarkable how his drawings bring it to life. He hopes this is just the beginning of his career.

Max states, *"I have been drawing since late 2008 and have continually improved my artwork over the years. My artistic inspiration comes from a variety of talented individuals such as Dr. Seuss, Don Bluth, Maurice Sendak, Peter De Seve, Graeme Base, Aaron Blaise, and Susio. These artists have influenced my style and creativity in different ways, leading me to develop a unique and diverse body of work."*

The Story of Womberg

In the Big Forest of Galoo, Womberg the Tyrannosaurus Rex is brushing his teeth with Beezle Beast Beetle toothpaste in The Blue Terry Tavern Lagoon.

As he rinses his mouth with a big gulp of water, he watches the water running down the mountain stream. He could see a Momma deer with her babies sipping water from the stream, and the first rays of sunlight were peeking out above the mountain in the distance.

As Womberg stretches his muscular green legs and his not-so-big arms, he decides to take a walk to look for some new friends. He walks through the plush green forest and hears a babbling brook in the distance.

Bird Buddies

As Womberg travels through the forest, he hears birds chirping and singing as they fly from branch to branch. He smiles as he watches the colorful birds greet another new day with fun and games. He is happy that these birds are terrific buddies and can spend the day playing games and singing with each other.

He decides that he must search the forest to find a buddy to have fun with. He smiles because he knows there are many animals in the Forest of Galoo, and one of them will be his new best friend so that he can have fun every day, just like these birds do.

10 Beavers

After walking a few more steps, he sees 10 beavers chewing twigs and moving mud paddies to build a big, strong dam. As he approaches the busy beavers, he asks the one in charge, "Hello! My name is Womberg the T-Rex. Do you want to be friends with me?"

Benny the Beaver Chief looks up at the green T-Rex with orange spots and replies, "We are way too busy to make friends today. Besides, you do not look like you are able to help us build a dam. Your arms are very tiny, your teeth are too sharp, and your tail is not flat."

Womberg is disappointed. He knows that he would be a good friend if someone gave him a chance. He decides to continue walking through the Big Forest of Galoo.

9 Zebras

As he approached the Savannah, he saw 9 Zebras eating brush and drinking out of the watering hole. He was hopeful, while the beavers were very busy, the zebras did not seem to be working too hard.

Womberg put a big smile on his face and walked up to the Zebra chief. "Hello, my name is Womberg the T-Rex, I would like to be your friend, what do you say?" Zack the head Zebra, shook his head and snorted at the green giant, "You are too big and too green to be our friend. All the lions and tigers and bears would be able to spot us from a mile away. Our stripes, hide us from these hungry beasts and help us to not be eaten by them at night. Go somewhere else, Lizard breath."

Womberg held back his tears, he knew that they were right. The zebras surely would stick out in the savannah with a Green T-Rex as part of the group.

Womberg gazed way up into the trees of the forest. He looked at all the feathered birds up in the branches of the tall trees. As he was walking under the branches of a tall pine tree, he saw a beautiful Red McCaw. He then saw a few more birds in the trees. Each McCaw was brighter than the next, in blue, yellow, green, and orange colors.

8 Macaws

He looked at his green and orange skin and got an idea. Maybe he could fit in with this flock of birds, and not stick out so much in the forest if he joined their group of 8 McCaws.

He decided to give it a try. "I am Womberg the giant green T-Rex, Do you birds want to be buddies with me.?" All the birds flapped their wings and squawked in a piercing tone.

Mickey the Main McCaw yelled above the noise, "Big Green, you will break all the branches we sit on. Besides, you can not even fly. All of our friends must fly to be in our band of birds." "Sorry, you cannot join our group. But we do like your orange spots. You are very colorful, just like us."

7 Koalas

Before Womberg could be sad about the McCaws rejecting his friendship, he saw movement in another tree about 100 yards away. He walked closer to get a better look. As he approached the Ginormas tree, way up at the top he saw a rolly polly figure. There were 7 Koalas eating and nesting in the trees. Keith the King Koala shouted down to Womberg. "Hey you, Big Green. Can you stop shaking the ground with your GIANT steps. You are knocking my COLONY of Koalas out of the trees."

Womberg did not realize that in his excitement to see his new friends that he was taking Giant steps that shook the ground and rattled the trees. Womberg was embarrassed and told King Keith that he apologized for his blunder. "I'm sorry for shaking the ground so much. I did not want any of your COLONY to fall from the trees. I really like Koala bears. Do you want to be friends if I promise to walk gently?"

"We are a friendly Colony, and get along well with all the animals. But I must deny your request of friendship. You are a menacing creature and I fear that your clumsy actions may knock over our trees or break our branches. This would endanger our colony and our friends and I cannot put our koalas at risk to call you a friend."

6 Rattlesnakes

Womberg could not believe his misfortune. He realized the King was right. He did not want to harm the Koalas and he did let his excitement shake them up so they did not feel safe. Womberg began walking further down the path through the forest. After a little while he heard a soft rattling noise. Looking up at a tree to investigate he suddenly saw the branches move. He realized that these were not just branches but RATTLESNAKES wrapped around the branches. Womberg spotted Ronnan the Reigning Rattler and asked,

"Would you and your DEN of 6 Rattlesnakes want to be friends with me?" Ronnan hissed at his bed of snakes and said, "Come closer Womberg, let me see you better." Womberg complied, and realized that he had been tricked by Ronnan. The Snake Leader jumped from the branch and wrapped 3 times around Womberg's snout staring with his demon eyes directly at Womberg. At Ronnan's command he felt rattlers start to climb up his legs. Then he felt more on his back, and another one on his arm. Ronnan commanded his Den to "Squeeze him tight." The rattlesnakes tried to squeeze Womberg tight to bring him down. What Ronnan did not realize is his 20-foot snakes were too short to get around the Giant Lizard.

Womberg realized these snakes were not his friend, but were trying to squeeze the life out of him for their next meal. He shook his head, his feet, and his tail sending the rattlers flying in all directions. Womberg then used his tail to grab one of the rattlers and shook him side to side to let him know his attack was fruitless. Womberg said, "You snakes are Evil and not to be trusted." Hissing back at him, Ronnan said, "All snakes are sneaky, and we would like a good meal, but a Lizard cannot be our friend." Womberg, hurling the last snake with his tail, then hurried away from this pit of rattlers and escaped in one piece.

The T-Rex knew he was lucky that the rattlesnakes were so small and could not harm him. But he still wanted to give friendship with all animals another try. He heard a familiar sound like crickets growing louder and louder as he headed deeper into the forest. Ribbit, Ribbit, Ribbit rang in his ears. In the darkness, he saw bright green eyes staring back at him.

Suddenly, a Tree frog landed on his snout and was staring directly back at him. "Hi, I'm Fritz the Tree Frog. What is a Giant Green Lizard doing in the deep forest?" Womberg smiled back at the Treefrog. "My name is Womberg, and I am looking to make new friends. Do you tree frogs like to play and have a fun time?"

5 Tree Frogs

Fun? We can't wait to have a fun time! With that the 5 Tree Frogs started jumping from the trees on to Wombergs head, shoulders and back. 1 tree frog slid down Womberg's tail and went flying into the air. Another tree frog did flips off T-Rex's head and dove into a puddle of water near his feet. And still a third tree frog bounced off the Green lizard's big belly and landed into a patch of soft clover.

Womberg was first happy that the tree frogs were having a good time. He was glad that they were not trying to attack him like the rattlers tried to do. But then he thought about it and realized he did not want to be treated like a GIANT JUNGLE JIM either by these over active reptiles. He decided he needed to keep on looking for friends. He shook his tail, and a tree frog when flying. Then he wiggled his head and his arms and his legs and the other frogs shook loose. Womberg continued his search for friendship. After 30 minutes of walking Womberg passed a swampy lake area. He decided this would be a great place to take a rest. It had been a long day and his feet were sore. He grabbed a branch with giant green leaves. He looked for a grassy area to sit down and he started to nibble on the leaves. As he settled down and wiggled his toes he felt EYES staring at him. He felt it but he could not see them. As he walked further, he spun around to catch the EYE holders looking at him. Sure enough, he saw 4 Heads pop out of the water and then quickly submerge.

4 Turtles

He realized that they were 4 Turtles spying on him, and he waited for them to pop their head up from the water to take a breath of fresh air. As Terrence the Top Turtle came up for air, Womberg gave him a great big smile and asked, "Hi, Mr. Turtle, can I be your friend?"

Terence the Top Turtle replied to Womberg, "Mr. Lizard, we love your beautiful GREEN color. You look like a GIANT version of us with NO SHELL." But we spend most of our time under water in our swampy lake. We swim, we crawl, we sleep, we eat and we stay underwater most of the time. If you jumped into our tiny lake, you would create a TIDAL WAVE 20 feet tall. All of our friends that live in the lake would be ship wrecked on shore and in the weeds.

Womberg said I am disappointed, but he knew he could not jump & swim & play in the lake without disrupting all the creatures that live in the lake. He knew Terrance was right and being friends with the turtles was not in the cards.

As the day passed, it started to get darker in the Forest. Womberg could not believe that the trees of the forest blocked out any light from the sunset. It was really dark now. With out the light, every sound of the forest and the animals became amplified. Sounds of crikets, and snakes and other animals filled the air. Womberg looked up in the branches and saw BIG BRIGHT EYES staring at him as he moved down the path.

He was not worried because he was always ready to make a new friend. Who did these eyes belong to. The eyes seemed to move from one branch to another. Sometimes he saw 2 eyes, other times 4 or 6 eyes. He then heard a low growl, turn into a roar. The sound got louder and louder as the other animals joined in. Who was trying to scare him?

3 Panthers

Peter the Primary Panther showed his face in the moonlight and growled out a command to Womberg. "Stop where you are or we will POUNCE on YOU!" The 3 Panthers now displayed their massive claws and Knifelike teeth as they all growled at Womberg. Follow my command or you will DIE!" Womberg was not scared, he retorted. "I will stop at your command. I do not want to fight. I am looking for friends, Do you POWERFUL PANTHERS want to be friends?"

The primary panther was confused by Womberg's request. Most animals in the forest were scared of the Powerful panthers. They would tremble in fear, not ask to be friends. Peter did not understand how this very big Green Lizard with orange spots could be so cool.

He responded back to Womberg, "Panthers have fun by ruling the forest. We patrol the savannah to make sure all the animals live in harmony. If anyone makes trouble we put them in their place. We control all the animals except the Elephants the Rhinos and the Hippos. We are too small to control them."

Peter stated, "We would be your friend if you would use your Huge jaws and gigantic teeth to scare these animals so we can rule over them. That would give us more power and make us VERY HAPPY. What do you say Womberg, Let's be friends." Womberg was shocked. Even though he was a Giant, he was a friendly beast. He would never terrorize any other animals. Elephants, Rhinos and Hippos were his friends. How could he be mean to them. They were never mean to him and Womberg does not like scaring anyone.

He told the Powerful Panthers, " I always look for friendship, but I never look to hurt my friends or any other animals. I'm sorry, I want to be your friend but I cannot be mean to any animals on the savannah. I cannot be your friend if that is what you want me to do." The panthers knew they were outmatched by Womberg's Giant size and big teeth. They disappeared into the night and Womberg knew they were gone.

2 Clown fish

Womberg continued his search for friendship. But that would have to wait till morning. It was late, he was tired, and he decided that he would sleep by the stream. The grassy field offered a comfortable place to lie down. The view of the stars made Womberg smile, he closed his eyes, and listened to the water roll gently down the stream.

The next morning, Womberg rolled over and stretched his ginormous green limbs. As he opened his eyes, he let out a gigantic roar. He made his way to the stream to get a drink of water. Womberg always started his mornings brushing his teeth. But first, he would get a drink of water to quench his thirst from not drinking all night while he slept. As Womberg lowered his giant jaw into the stream, he felt the cool water dance through his teeth and over his tongue. He took a massive gulp of water and raised his head to swallow his big gulp of refreshing water. As he prepared to swallow the cold, refreshing liquid, he felt something flap against his massive tongue. Then he felt it hit the back of his throat. Womberg got scared and started to choke. He coughed and coughed as he gasped for air.

As a reflex, he spit out all the water back into the stream. Then he splashed more water into his mouth and started to gargle. Finally, he rinsed his mouth out again. The giant lizard looked down at the stream to see if he could tell what he almost swallowed. He saw two tiny orange-and-white fish swimming around his legs trying to get his attention. Womberg submerged his head and came face to face with two clown fish that were very angry at him. "How dare you try to eat us," the tiny scaled creature exclaimed. Caleb and Cory the Clown Fish stared straight into Womberg's eyes.

Womberg was surprised that these tiny clown fish caused him to choke on a gulp of water. "I am so sorry, I had no idea that I almost swallowed you when I was taking my morning drink of water. Had I known you were swimming there, I certainly would have gulped water somewhere else." He apologized. "You tried to eat me for breakfast, you horrible green monster! You have terrible breath, and I am not your morning appetizer." Womberg asked a question. "Are you too mad at me to be my friend? I do not want you for a snack. I want you for a friend."

The clown fish stared at each other in disbelief. "We do not want to be your friend. You almost swallowed us whole. We cannot be friends with you because we do not drink water, we live and swim in water. You are a giant dragon that could eat us in one gulp. You are not a good friend for a fish!" With that, Caleb and Cory blew bubbles at Womberg and swam off to deeper depths in the stream.

1 Mouse

Womberg was sad. He did not mean to hurt the little fish. He only wanted a drink of water and to brush his teeth. He got out his Beezle Beast Beetle toothpaste and started brushing his ginormous teeth. The Green giant double-checked to make sure that there were no fish that he may swallow by mistake.

Womberg walked along the stream and was happy to have another day to find friends. He sat down on a rock beside the grassy trail to take a rest. He liked the warm sun heating up his tail and the cool breeze against his scaly face. As he stared down at the grass, he noticed an ANT HILL filled with busy ants carrying crumbs and leaves into the ant hill. Womberg looked at the ants and wondered why they have so many friends all living together in that ant hill and he could not find one friend. He thought of all the reasons he could not have friends. He did not have a flat tail, or black and white stripes. He also was too big to sit in a tree without breaking the branches. He was too huge to swim without making a tidal wave.

All the animals did not want his friendship. He heard no from beavers, zebras, macaws, koalas, rattlesnakes, tree frogs, turtles, panthers, and clownfish. He said out loud, "I might NEVER find ANY animal that wants to be a friend to a Giant Green Dinosaur. I might just have to accept that I am going to be on my own forever and ever."
Suddenly, he felt two small feet walking up his tail. A voice from behind him said, "Hey Big Green, I can be your friend." Mandrel the Mouse advised, "I can make that happen. Yep, you seem to be a nice guy… Very big, but very Nice! You see your problem is that you want to be friends with animals that travel in packs and tribes, and herds. You need someone who is ALONE, Just Like you."

"Well, let me tell you, Opposites attract."
"You are Big and I am Small. But I am big enough to ride on your gigantic big shoulders."
"You have big eyes and I have small eyes, but I can see farther than you, and I can spot danger a mile away."
"You are loud when you take your giant steps, but I am quiet like a mouse. I can sneak around to find us food and drink."
"You are green and I am brown and red. You blend into the forest, and I blend into the savannah."
"You are a Lizard and I am a mammal."
"We are different and that is good."

1 Buddy by Your Side

As Womberg walks through the forest with Mandrel on his shoulder, all the animals notice the pair. They see the bond between the giant green T-Rex and the tiny red mouse and smile in admiration. The beavers stop building their dam, the zebras pause at their watering hole, and even the macaws squawk in amazement. The koalas peek down from their trees, the rattlesnakes watch silently, and the panthers observe from the shadows.

Each animal realizes that Womberg has finally found what he was searching for all along—a true friend. Some of them offer apologies for turning him away, but Womberg responds kindly, "A good team is worth waiting for."

With Mandrel as his buddy, Womberg feels confident and happy. The pair walks along the stream, ready for new adventures. They decide to share their friendship with all the animals of the forest, whether they're big or small, swimmers or flyers, carnivores or vegetarians.

"Life is always better with a buddy by your side," Womberg says with a wide grin as they journey into the distance.

www.ingramcontent.com/pod-product-compliance
Lightning Source LLC
Chambersburg PA
CBHW042107090526

44590CB00004B/119